GOLDILOCKS

Written By Leslie Falconer   Pictures By Chris Lensch

A special thanks goes to my son Olan.
His imagination sent Goldilocks on a
whole new adventure! -C.L.

First published by Experience Early Learning Company
7243 Scotchwood Lane, Grawn, Michigan 49637 USA

ISBN: 978-1-937954-24-6
Visit us at www.ExperienceEarlyLearning.com

GOLDILOCKS

Written By Leslie Falconer   Pictures By Chris Lensch

Goldilocks loved Baby Bear.
They did everything together.

They ate snacks.

They read books.

They played hide-and-seek.

They did everything together.
Everything, that is, except
clean up.

One day, Baby Bear disappeared.
Goldilocks looked everywhere,
but everywhere was a big mess.

It was a mess on the table.
It was a mess on the chair.
It was a mess on her bed.

5

Goldilocks cried herself to sleep.
Her bear was lost.

"I have to find Baby Bear," Goldilocks said as she ran into the dark woods of her dream.

She came upon a cottage built into
the trunk of a great oak tree.
The door was open.
Maybe Baby Bear was inside?

So Goldilocks peeked inside and saw...

...a mess! Even if Baby Bear was here, she would never be able to find him.

So she set about tidying up the cottage. She started with a pile of dirty dishes on the table.

Goldilocks quickly washed the dishes and set them nicely back onto the table. Then she organized the rest of the room, all the while hoping she might find Baby Bear.

Just as she finished, she saw a mess of books stacked on three chairs. There were so many books on the smallest chair that it had fallen apart.

Goldilocks fixed the small chair, and then she put the books neatly away.

Still, she did not find her bear.

14

As Goldilocks looked up from the books, she saw a long, mysterious staircase.

She wondered what was at the top. Could Baby Bear be up there?

She tiptoed up the stairs and saw...

16

...another mess! Blankets, pillows and clothes were all over the floor! Maybe Baby Bear was here, but she could not see him.

So Goldilocks shook out the blankets and carefully made the beds. Next, she fluffed the pillows until they were as soft as clouds, and finally she put the clothes away.

Exhausted from cleaning, Goldilocks decided to take a little nap.

As she was sleeping, three bears arrived home from a day of picking berries.

19

"Someone's been washing my dirty dishes," exclaimed Papa Bear.

"Someone's been washing my dirty dishes too," said Mama Bear.

"Someone's been washing my dirty dishes and nicely set the table!" said Baby Bear.

20

The bears clapped their
paws in happiness.

"And look," said Papa Bear, "someone has been cleaning up the books on my chair."
"Someone's been cleaning up the books on my chair too," said Mama Bear.

"Someone's been cleaning up the books on my chair and even fixed the broken leg," said Baby Bear. Baby Bear jumped into his chair with a big smile.

But the bears were confused.

who had cleaned up their mess?
When they noticed that their
bedroom door upstairs was open,
they decided to investigate.

They bumbled up the stairs and Papa Bear exclaimed, "Someone's been folding the blankets on my bed." "Someone's been folding the blankets on my bed too," said Mama Bear. "Someone's been folding the blankets on my bed and is sleeping on my pillow right now!" exclaimed Baby Bear.

Just then, Goldilocks woke up and saw...

...Baby Bear!

GOLDILOCKS

W
A B
C Z

experience
EARLY LEARNING

Experience Early Learning specializes in the development and publishing of research-based curriculum, books, music and authentic assessment tools for early childhood teachers and parents around the world. Our mission is to inspire children to experience learning through creative expression, play and open-ended discovery. We believe educational materials that invite children to participate with their whole self (mind, body and spirit) support on-going development and encourage children to become the authors of their own unique learning stories.

www.ExperienceEarlyLearning.com